Dawnette Meredith and Brittney Mere[...]

Illustrated by Ashley Kochn[...]

AWeSoMe OLLie

Ollie is a real bear – a real Teddy Bear that is...

Ollie educates and encourages people living with an ostomy to live joyful, boundless lives. Ollie feels awesome thanks to his red button stoma and removable ostomy pouch. This is his story.

To purchase, sponsor, or read more about Awesome Ollie the Teddy Bear visit:

AwesomeOstomy.com

ISBN-13: 978-0692091531 (Daisy Press)
ISBN-10: 069209153X

To my family – the treasure of my lifetime.

—Ephesians 3:20

Thanks to

The United Ostomy Associations of America and Ostomy
Nurses everywhere for all you do to improve the lives of
people living with ostomies.

Ollie the bear is awake with the sun,

imagining ways to make the day fun.

He noodles and doodles, and makes lots of plans,

to play with his friends for as long as he can.

This little bear loves to run, jump, and swing
but he takes lots of breaks, because of one thing:

Often his tummy will have a bad day,
with too many "ouches" to go out and play.

Ollie the bear has been feeling so glum,

for being a cub is no fun with his tum!

He's tried a few things, but short of a cure,

he made an appointment to see Doctor Fur.

Fur looked and he listened from bottom to top,
from floor paws to eyeballs to tummy- and stopped.

He listened and squinted, and then got a clue.

"Don't worry," he said, "I know what to do!"

The doctor showed Ollie a colorful chart,
to show how he'd get Ollie's tum to restart.

The Doctor told Ollie that soon he could play

without fear of the "ouches"—he'd take them away!

Ollie skipped and he sang down the hallway with glee,

he high-fived the doctor before surgery.

The nice nurse gave Ollie a blue gown and cap,
put Ollie in bed and said "have a nice nap!"

Ollie woke up just a little bit sore,

and felt somewhat different than he did before.

The nice nurse came by to see how he was feeling.

"Maybe an ice pop will help with the healing?"

When Doctor Fur visited early that day,

He assured that the soreness would soon go away.

The doctor uncovered his little blue gown,
and on Ollies tum, something new could be found!

The doctor made Ollie a little red button.

He heard it start gurgling all of the sudden!

"Hey, look at my button and fancy new cover!"

So many new things for this bear to discover.

"The button's a stoma," the doctor told Ollie.

It's red and it's squishy and struck him so oddly.

The stoma is wrapped in a pocket or pouch,

so Ollie could potty without saying "ouch!"

He wondered a few times how long he must stay,
so Fur could be sure that his tum was okay.

But Ollie was hopeful the pouch did the trick,
and he could go play soon without feeling sick!

Surprised by some grumbling early one morning,

His potty came out without even a warning.

His stoma and pouch did a marvelous job.

The potty came out without pinches or throbs.

His pouch holds the potty- a curious feat!

Ollie thought to himself, "my button is neat!"

Ollie the bear is quite awesome, he'd say.

Because he now pottys uniquely his way.

Ollie the bear can still run, jump, and swing.

Why, this fuzzy bear cub can do anything!

His tummy is happy and doesn't say "ouch!"

All thanks to his ostomy button and pouch.

Resources

AwesomeOstomy.com
Home of Awesome Ollie the Teddy Bear with an Ostomy. Strategies and Resources for Living with an Ostomy.

United Ostomy Association of America
https://www.ostomy.org/
The United Ostomy Associations of America, Inc. (UOAA) is a 501(c)(3) nonprofit organization that supports, empowers,and advocates for people who have had or who will have ostomy or continent diversion surgery

Ostomy at Home - YouTube
https://www.youtube.com/watch?v=eLmfXLy4wa0
Published on Dec 9, 2015
Experts at Primary Children's Hospital created this video to help parents and families care for a child's ostomy at home. This video will teach you about normal digestion, types of ostomies, ostomy pouches and how to empty them, how to change an ostomy pouch, skin care with ostomies, daily care tips, eating to stay healthy, and problems that may occur with an ostomy.

Hospital Mom Hacks- YouTube
Helpful hints from a medical mom

Miracle Snappies
Adaptive, custom made snappy clothing for your child's medical special needs.
http://www.facebook.com/miraclesnappies Can also be found on Etsy

Association for the Bladder Exstrophy Community (A-BE-C)
https://www.bladderexstrophy.com/
A community to ensure that all who are affected by bladder exstrophy have the opportunity to realize their greatest life purpose and potential.

Oley Foundation
http://oley.org/
Striving to enrich the lives of those living with home intravenous nutrition and tube feeding through education, advocacy, and networking.

Pull Through Network
http://www.pullthrunetwork.org/
Information, Education, Support and Advocacy for Families, Children, Teens and Adults Who Are Living With The Challenges of Congenital Anorectal, Colorectal or Urogenital Disorders

Youth Rally
http://www.youthrally.org/
To provide an environment for adolescents living with conditions of the bowel and bladder that encourages self-confidence and independent living.

About the Authors

Dawnette Meredith grew up in the farm communities of Indiana and attended Indiana University. She now works and lives with her husband in Southern California, where she raised three children.

She underwent ostomy surgery in December of 2015, resulting in a permanent colostomy. Her surgery ignited a passion to encourage and empower ostomates of all ages to live confident beautifully full lives. She wrote this book as a message to the young and the young at heart, that life with an ostomy is limitless.

Dawnette is the Founder and creator of Awesome Ollie and the Big Bear Project. Ollie Teddy bears have stomas and ostomy pouches and are given to children in the United States and Canada who undergo ostomy surgery. Awesome Ollie has been featured at the National UOAA Conference, Ostomy Canada magazine, Phoenix magazine and OstomyConnection.com

Her journey to find out how to live life abundantly with an ostomy brought her in connection with the United Ostomy Association, medical experts and other ostomates, and now she dedicates her life as a patient advocate. She is also the founder of AwesomeOstomy.com and shares practical lifestyle strategies for living with an ostomy through her informative video blog. Many of her videos have gone international.

Brittney Meredith received her Bachelor's Degree in Nursing from San Diego State University in 2016. Since then, she has worked as a gastrointestinal nurse in northern San Diego County. She was thrilled to be part of this project, as it combines some of her greatest loves: patient education/empowerment and the creative arts! Working on this project with her mom and giggling over the developing rhymes and sketches are memories she will treasure. Brittney is so proud of her Mom's personal journey and the passion she has put into advocating for people with ostomies all around the world.

Manufactured by Amazon.ca
Acheson, AB

13781377R00021